STARTERS
SCIENCE

KU-376-283

WITHDRAWN
FROM STOCK

Light
and Shadows

Macdonald Educational

The sun gives us light.
Bright sunshine makes clear shadows.

FIFE EDUCATIONAL
RESOURCES CENTRE

Look at the shadows on a cloudy day.
Are they the same on a sunny day?

Everything makes shadows.
Look at the different shapes.
4

paper

Make your shadow into different shapes.
Draw round your friend's shadow.
You can cut the shapes out of paper.

5

Try making shadow shapes like these
with your friends.

6

Let your shadow fall against a wall
or a car.
What happens to its shape?

What shadow shapes will these make?
Move each one until you make
the largest and smallest shadow you can.
Try some other things.

8

Try making shadows of things with holes.
Cut different shaped holes in paper.
Does a bubble make a shadow?

9

These children have drawn round
a shadow in the morning, at lunchtime,
and in the evening.
Try this for yourselves.
10

sundials

These are some sundials.
On sunny days the shadow tells the time.
You can make a sundial with a stick.
Mark where the shadow falls every hour.

11

You can play shadow tag.
Try to touch someone else's shadow
with your foot or your own shadow.
12

shadow
bird

You can make shadow animals
with your hands.
Make them move.
Use sunlight or a bright lamp.

13

card

stick

brass paper fastener

Cut some puppet shapes out of card.
Fix them to sticks.
14

You can give a shadow puppet show.

Plants need light.
See how plants grow towards the window.
16

Crowded trees grow up tall
to reach the light.
Very little grows in the shade
underneath their branches.

These plants grow in sunny places.

18

These plants grow in shady places.

Some things shine more than others.
This means they reflect light well.
What things can you see in the picture
that reflect light well?

20

The moon reflects light from the sun.

FIFE EDUCATIONAL
RESOURCES CENTRE   JS3S

21

Hold a mirror in different positions.
What do you see?
Can you see round corners?

Reflect a spot of sunlight with a mirror.
Can you make it follow a line?
You can play light-spot tag
with a friend.

Hold your right hand up to the mirror.
Which hand does your reflection hold up?
24

trick mirrors

car mirror

shaving or
makeup mirror

Curved mirrors can make funny shapes.
Some curved mirrors are very useful.
They can make things look bigger
or smaller.

25

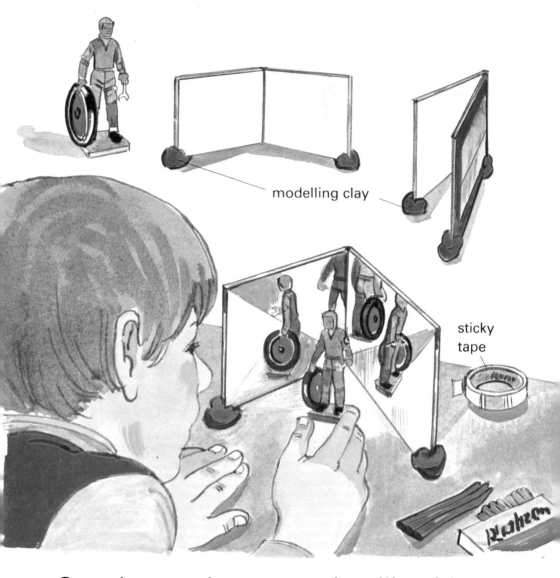

modelling clay

sticky tape

Stand two mirrors together like this.
Put a small toy between them.
Move the mirrors further apart.
What do you see now?
26

sticky tape

Stand three small mirrors together.
Put some small, brightly coloured things
in one corner.
What patterns can you make?

Index

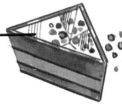
FIFE EDUCATIONAL
RESOURCES CENTRE